Una red para pescar

por Jessica Quilty

Scott Foresman
is an imprint of

PEARSON

Glenview, Illinois • Boston, Massachusetts • Chandler, Arizona
Upper Saddle River, New Jersey

Every effort has been made to secure permission and provide appropriate credit for photographic material. The publisher deeply regrets any omission and pledges to correct errors called to its attention in subsequent editions.

Unless otherwise acknowledged, all photographs are the property of Pearson.

Photo locations denoted as follows: Top (T), Center (C), Bottom (B), Left (L), Right (R), Background (Bkgd)

Opener: ©Michael S. Yamashita/CORBIS; 1 ©Anthony Bannister; Gallo Images/CORBIS; 3 ©Michael Freeman/CORBIS; 4 ©Michael S. Yamashita/CORBIS; 6 ©Julie Habel/CORBIS; 7 ©Anthony Bannister; Gallo Images/CORBIS; 8 ©Phil Schermeister/CORBIS

ISBN 13: 978-0-328-53419-7
ISBN 10:   0-328-53419-6

Copyright © by Pearson Education, Inc., or its affiliates. All rights reserved. Printed in the United States of America. This publication is protected by copyright, and permission should be obtained from the publisher prior to any prohibited reproduction, storage in a retrieval system, or transmission in any form or by any means, electronic, mechanical, photocopying, recording, or likewise. For information regarding permissions, write to Pearson Curriculum Rights & Permissions, One Lake Street, Upper Saddle River, New Jersey 07458.

Pearson® is a trademark, in the U.S. and/or other countries, of Pearson plc or its affiliates.

Scott Foresman® is a trademark, in the U.S. and/or other countries, of Pearson Education, Inc., or its affiliates.

2 3 4 5 6 7 8 9 10 V0N4 13 12 11 10

¡Estos pescadores acaban de encontrar muchos peces!

Los pescadores tiran el ancla y luego echan sus redes en alta mar. Tienen que esperar durante un rato. Los peces nadan hacia las redes, y cuando están completamente llenas, los pescadores las jalan. Después, regresan a la playa.

Muchos pescadores venden lo que pescan a grandes clientes. Otros llevan el pescado a sus casas para comer. Mañana muchos pescadores volverán a hacer el mismo trabajo.

Ahora piensa en esto: ¿En qué crees que se parece una red de pescador a una telaraña?

La araña teje su telaraña con hilo de seda. ¿Crees que es verdad que una araña pequeñita puede construir algo así? ¡Claro que sí!

La araña tiene hambre después de tanto trabajo. Por eso se come todo lo que atrapó o "pescó" en su telaraña.